2nd Grade Handwriting:
Beginners Cursive Workbook

Speedy Publishing LLC
40 E. Main St. #1156
Newark, DE 19711
www.speedypublishing.com

astronomy

the scientific study of stars, planets, and other objects in outer space

astronomy   *astronomy*

besides

other than (someone or something)

besides   besides

bounce

to cause to hit against a surface and quickly move in a different and usually opposite direction

bounce   *bounce*

connect

to join (two or more things) together

connect   *connect*

dangerous

involving possible injury, harm, or death : characterized by danger

dangerous　　　*dangerous*

dozen

a group of 12 people or things

dozen   *dozen*

excess

an amount that is more than the usual or necessary amount

excess   *excess*

famous

known or recognized by very many people : having fame

famous *famous*

frighten

to cause (someone) to become afraid

frighten   *frighten*

gravity

the natural force that tends to cause physical things to move towards each othe

gravity *gravity*

instrument

a tool or device used for a particular purpose

instrument   *instrument*

lonely

sad from being apart from other people

lonely   *lonely*

luxury

a condition or situation of great comfort, ease, and wealth

luxury   *luxury*

mention

a short statement about something or someone :
an act of mentioning something or someone

mention   mention

nervous

having or showing feelings of being worried and afraid about what might happen

parade

a public celebration of a special day or event that usually includes many people and groups

parade   *parade*

present

something presented

present   present

rumor

information or a story that is passed from person to person but has not been proven to be true

rumor   *rumor*

scholar

a person who has studied a subject for a long time and knows a lot about it

scholar   *scholar*

shelter

a structure that covers or protects people or things

shelter   *shelter*

shiver

one of the small pieces into which a brittle thing is broken by sudden violence

shiver   *shiver*

support

to agree with or approve of (someone or something)

support　　　*support*

telescope

a device shaped like a long tube that you look through in order to see things that are far away

telescope   telescope

tremble

to shake slightly because you are afraid, nervous, excited, etc.

tremble   tremble

wealthy

having a lot of money and possessions

whisper

to speak very softly or quietly

whisper   *whisper*

wonder

something or someone that is very surprising, beautiful, amazing, etc.

wonder　　*wonder*

worry

to think about problems or fears : to feel or show fear and concern

worry   worry

zigzag

a line that has a series of short, sharp turns or angles